afterlove

MARIO PETRUCCI

Cinnamon Press
:: small miracles from distinctive voices ::

Published by Cinnamon Press
Meirion House
Tanygrisiau
Blaenau Ffestiniog
Gwynedd, LL41 3SU
www.cinnamonpress.com

ISBN: 978-1-78864-095-4

British Library Cataloguing in Publication Data. A CIP record for this book can be obtained from the British Library.

Designed and typeset in Times New Roman by Cinnamon Press.

Cover design by Adam Craig. Cover image unearthed by the author.

Cinnamon Press is represented in the UK by Inpress Ltd and in Wales by the Books Council of Wales.

Acknowledgements

Lazarus was previously published in *Eighty Four: Poems on Male Suicide, Vulnerability, Grief and Hope* (Verve Poetry Press, 2019; ed. Helen Calcutt); *holy* previously appeared online in B O D Y (bodyliterature.com, 12th August 2013). *our bluest Drop* owes a debt to Daniel Ladinsky's *A Suspended Blue Ocean*.

When it comes to those we love, even our most yearned-for states of union are subject to change. *afterlove* endures the swarming devastations of loss as consummately as it enters love's raptures, ever alive to devotion's flow and ebb. From domestic paean centred on the beloved, through a father's unabashed affection for his children, to the sometimes savage realisations of love's dissolution, these poems succeed in spanning relationship heaven and hell. Mario Petrucci generates love (and non-love) poetry that refuses to squint in the glare of experience. With characteristic candour and inventiveness, whether through light-filled lyric or a murderous remaking of myth, Petrucci takes us just about everywhere love can go.

afterlove is a collection marked by emotional openness and imaginative risk. These poems of family connection and disconnection are probing, and those featuring the poet's relationship to his children are particularly striking in their tenderness and honesty.

Moniza Alvi

Contents

*

afterlove

They

They want me to speak of You.
I say: Wherever You walk is deep
with Paradise. When they meet
my gaze: You're pacing there.

I take moon as kindred type: so far
yet graceful; such yellowy ripeness.
I climb the slates, spread dark arms
to make a star – claim Your likeness.

So there is no Truth? they protest. *No
Lie?* I describe Your eyes. They want
proof of the aroma of clouds. I suggest
they bury their face in Your curls.

Burning, they ask: *You say you
returned from your grave?* I kiss them
as You first kissed me – on the mouth
with that fierce tenderness of a Saviour.

They insist: *Make this mist
reveal the sun.* Because they are
serious, I loosen my clothes as
You have done. Undress.

They frown: *Who on this hallowed
Earth do you think you are?* I run a thumb
down my crease of brow – show Your
narrow path that fetched me here.

Slyly they single out a wretch
destroyed by Love. In joy, I verify:
Without a living doubt – yes
this is Your work.

As last resort they argue:
How can this minion be divine?
I trace no thought with my reply.
Place in each palm a lit candle.

Still they persist: *We're separate!*
I send them resisting to my chambers.
If there they hear infectious cries of Love,
they will be ours. Such a cry forever lingers.

Beloved, for those who wish – alone
and pure – to know: *How? When? Why? If?*
I let these lips reply as if to Yours: *Like
this. Like this. Like this.*

Oh— that cloudless moonless night you danced
near-naked in phosphorescent shallows

Slim body shadowed to a trance : hallowed dark
boned against aglow-dark whose stars

Lost in your laughter glinted brighter— edged
in for a closer look— took you for One

of their Own.

it's how you

move
which is not so much
walking

as a way
of loving : a swaying in kind
with july

air wound
slyly shimmered towards & around
swarmed in

-visibles that
clamour to conquer you that contour
you as these

eyes do You
stooped at a car with one palm slack
reaching for

some dropped
thing in the back – all an act as
God as

eternal
matters no matter how
far

bend too

bath

I get in after you
our tub a flawless hulk scoured bald
clean-enamelled

indeed that whitest leanest ship powered
by its own containment steaming
sure and hard through

low half-light as I slip-slow in – this sanely
sudless shard of the Jurassic where
I scald myself gigantic

seeing suddenly everything inverted – all brine
its blood-warm cargo and our slight
boat ferrying it whose

buoyancy is that endless dearth through which our
nightly lozenge of ablution sails so
restlessly transparent

– such is this water you left alive that I plop me in
with that desire in a fish apparently
on the hook wishing

breathless return because this fluid with you has
been intimate: its druid mould that
keeps cold death out

adapting its magical fit to perfectly cling yet
wringing each from its anti-grave
in wingless effortless

rise: so here I lie eyes closed saving day's
unlit best till last as if this water
cooling were a body

at rest ready to depart in one upward
draught or what translates us
vapour to fearless

vapour in little slops and slaps –
or perhaps when I conflate
water with you

enpearled so clear
within it I see everything and
nothing of this world

what swells within

these cells in
pomegranate compartments
slitty seed

in tart juice
if not
You? your serum pent with form

bled through
my rapture superimposed as honey
delirious

on mead
– those soft grits unquenchable in me
pressed between

twinned stones
that wrench then hug across our surface
roundly ground

fearing all
will be rendered dully duly-flavoured
dust – though

You remain
musty grain of me dug into skyless
field sprouting

down this
forever-furrow my spine makes
: love

I
have shoved nib & blade
up to light

through You – am he
sprung
green from

your night rib
not You
from mine

storm

still
far off that
roil in light & dark

dankly
stratospheric
eyeliner to tree-lashed

horizon –
an oil-slick tension
swilling blue : not yet that

cough
thick & watery
slaughtering sky to earth but

ozone
off breezy skin that quickens
through

churned-grey vapours into
black as the air
slack in

me in its inverted bowl
grips
suddenly at an inner

sense as firming
cream
comes to hold all at

once &
at last its whipping shaft
tense with

rolling-in relief this light in
you
from blue-black tops a glow in

us
that shifts from over shoulders to
make you

crane &
arch your spine shuddered supple
along its length &

split from mine as a lash tossed
out &
up just before its downward

snap
until our breath in great
fat drops

slaps into our sunlit
dust your slow
slow

oh

& love

can one not speak
too plain in lines &
breaks

of what happens with
us
as dawn rounds a bend

in the river of this bed as
two blend twilight
beneath their obsidian lake

rising to an opened mouth to
kiss surface
till suppleness slips in sombre

brightness & milk-silver flicks
deep through dark back
to the depths

so
why not speak plainly of this?
that when unhidden

in white & black & half-lit
rooms I
fill you & you empty

me
I feel as the sea did
when Jesus

ate a fish from it

holy

&
what is really
so? this

body
alone in its cells or
your

curve
subtle in dawn & duvet
-sheathed

that fall
& swell of hills an almost
-light on

near-pitch
in fervour each for the other
unable to

breathe
such nights as elsewhere-sun
rises

lowly
-white while here all love &
desire

come
together in dark replete at
last breath

-less with
one body slow-breathed
to complete

their trinity

dawn face

yours &
mine I cannot
see without your now

expressionless mirror two
statues still alive side
by side

careful bodies
composed along their
tomb these grey folds of stone

softened for sleeplessness flows
bloodward to seize this
armoured man

old with
waiting who is not
supine looking to god through closed

lids but choosing in half-sleep to watch
his love sleeping – day's firm
lips drained

of tension
with teeth faintly bright in
dream those tiny shimmerings in lashes

as twilight swells through the room my
flint
slowly loosening until I seem pilgrim

to your chill cathedral who alone
gazes on the slimly lifelike
mouth an

hour then
feels as holy shock
the stony richness razing hotly

through when with morning
your once alabaster
cheek

twitches

mornings

whose photonic flood at the window
seems to one eye open
that last thinned

rinse from its glass
of bluish milk – sieved through
eyelids to a few dull thuds on each

underwater cell of retina
& what part of me asks if dawn is
this light at the window

or my alertness to it? or
how morning must wake a body
entire in all its red & white

hills and valleys
this cellular body coming to
life to light

like a mothering planet
turning
into the sun

one saw

by an Essex brook a capybara
so keenly still on windswept grass as if
a photograph of itself whose green blades shook

another spotted by her tumbledown shed three
flamingo sunset-struck making of necks
backward question marks

while a third swore the cobra timelessly
met her in a sudden thickening
of washing line

but I felt in my kitchen
at dusk a brow in black so
finely densely knit to inquisitive

touch such an eyebrow intricately more
miraculous than any coral reef then
sunless through the house

a red-lipped glimpse of teeth and I swear
I caught this deep unblinking
morning

your species of one
that never-to-be-extinct *you*
asleep in my bed

What you said

while I slept – quicksilver words
leapt one soul to another
decanted through whispers to sleeping ear

some part of me must have heard
like those tight lines of dust-light I saw before
eyes closed and I curved my back to you

smooth crescent of flesh snug to your flesh sea
and clothes floor-strewn dark with old lives
with late light sectoring hotel rug and wall

to fall on your cloud half-rose with sunset
I saw you in that mirror opposite
rise over me to vapour flush with dying sun

in that hotel we paid for with discoloured notes
our sum crumpled to monetary parts
our means crumpled in my palm like afterlove sheets

and I woke to you in another room washing
knowing you'd said something
something you'd never say to dark of day

words I carry now through the temporary
separatenesses life imposes like that blue
between white roses of cloud ever the same

or the way you stroke my cheek after love
when I return from work
uttering silence through voluble eyes

your brush of knuckles along my chin
so wildly tender as though to remake
my face a painting

as if I had never lover nor mother
this lover wordless with dawn
to stroke and speak her freshborn child

The Way you Look

in such light
just before dawn has
a hold: old light caressing your nape
undressing your face that
rinses you

for something drawn here hovers within you
between this light and this dark
a kiss of light that all but possesses your shape
so tenuous
and so all the more possessed

we are not speaking now
just breathing
and from night's lonely logic I woke
to your lovely breath – to our rhythm of breathing
fallen together as if
as we slept
two slow and sundered lovers totally unknown to us
had made of air one tender coming

and your face so bare
a moon in its heaven dim with blueness
held warm in this room with all that once imbued us
now shared in this space
between us

face of one unseen and painless
so powerfully asleep yet about to speak of gain
and loss
of how every tear must be drop to its lake
of everything – everything
somehow possible

And then you wake

§

for Kalina

lanugo

an interior
the size of a green
cantaloupe

you grow
on mother-sap to few
-ounced

fruit
strangely adrift in
dim

fields
able to lift that
kin-fist

as cellophane
skin
thickens with fat

simple Russian doll
about to be
real : you quicken

to Mozart – dart
with
Beethoven then

some low
-pitched Gaga ah
giga-celled

parasite yet
concealed we adore &
feed you still

seed-tight so
rich just beneath the navel
while once-

knarled papa
glides through mornings
as though he

were a sail
to work up dreams
for each

tinily
pearled toe-
nail

you dark

-eyed god
god-eyed whose
eyes brim dark you

look & suck then
suck & look
water

waters
drew down
through one current

-wise the lone moon at
your long-sailed
back

milk
through your
blood – webbed

liver
of placenta
your wobbling ship

come
goddess Come
mild

daughter
to the sun
tiny

scale
balancing mother
& your

fresh
-died sphincter
black

-eyed
bean of pink
see

fine
fingered
fire

of pain
pushed through
you

sweet
almond to this
womaned

tree

& if tonight

i died in
this
reaching over the waist

of a woman so light with
sleep
to the hand of a child

barely in this world
– conducting
her tiny shudders & shocks

around my thumb
as if
the mother-milk sucked

were something God
given
which it is

&
if a reach across the waist &
hips of a pitch

-haired woman
who names herself in freedom
my woman

to this
vibrant clasp of twitched
dark in a daughter's tiny grip

were my last
– then i could pass as
a christ

in a world that had no
need
for loss or nails bloodied

or crosses

in these arms

you sleep
small bright valley
unmined in my mountain fold

yet
through you old tremors
rise as though earth had seized your

spine a seam
through which to speak – little
seismometer

of what?
&
how

forgotten
already those veins in me
registering once

remotest swell
of speech as sleeplessness through
every sixth or

seventh breath
arrives upon your cliff as if each near-
waking were

miniature spring
reaching up in waves too fast too
wild from deep

-most beds to shake me into
finding means at last
to hush you

as one be
-calmed afternoon
wind found

a way with me to make
mild grass sigh
intelligibly

to my half
-gone child or breeze a
shush

through trees

little one

whose dawn palm
in my grasp seems a tensioned
underwater thing

finger-tight &
sinew-strung while new-found breath
bears you up

from sleep with
limbs in spate – plump-pink beetle firmly
on your back

carrion exposed
to slow-swooping light as though in you life
were rehearsing

all forms towards
life – until mother descends with cardigan out
-stretched a bat

black-flapped with
dark membranously huge to fuse collapse upon
the daughter as

suddenly all in
this world in sinful memory becomes less than
gauze first sun

made of wings that flew weakly
briefly through

daughter

I cut you
one tiny circus of cheese

: cheddar stronger than blood
I trace

in a circle at the tip of a blade &
place

upon your trusting tongue calling it
moon

to seize & bring you to this moment
all but

gone as soon as made – as though
far more

than mud & dust could sing us
as if this

softest planet I rest forever
almost

within your red space
of mouth

were *ah* now I
see it :

host

our bluest Drop

because of You
our sky
is Ocean in suspense

Stars
flick tails among the Souls
that swim

our every Planet : a white
whale You skim
upon so

Sun &
Moon may fuse to become
this – Your

heart
& Skin – in that truest
Sea

You have made us
let there Be
no rule

only One
Beloved do not
refuse

Your Own
deep
blue Drop – O

Thou
unschooled
so Unstoppably So :

be You
Bluest Love
Be

You

for Matteo

boy

in distress
who turns from my offered
kiss so

helpless
that long look lost behind the eyes
galaxies away

my hand this long arm of sand around
the small shoulder mere frost
warming cold

who put him in this world? whose wealth
of warmths should swarm him &
in the man he

even now becomes how
many breathlessnesses like these will he alone
keep to himself & with

me already far flown on my way to amicable
dust
will it console the burning man too slow

to heal his child to learn that even
distant stars about
to burst must one day feel?

Lineage

I see them now
behind me – dad drawing
long on a late evening fag

mum slumped
skew in her chair
her care-worn spirit
a gossamer

& my grandparents stand behind them &
the next generation behind those –
so the cascade goes
on & on

they fade bluely backwards
into a widening wake of desire
a precise swarm – an exact
multiple of two

& if any one of them should fall
any single one
everything before them falls

yet their flesh funnel
narrows down to me – this
hallowed sticking point
this temporary resistance

that opens again
to my own insistent children
to their children yet to come

I am this neck
of human hourglass – my
eternal moment pours minutely
these grains of life

son
daughter
we are never quite sand –
pass life on as I have done but
unwaning through more willing fingers
with more willing hands
pass it on

Rispetti

I

As light must, to itself, I wake to you, warm.
Long before we met, you lay beside me, here.
Soon, day will rouse itself. For now, matter firms
as these bodies' flung-together dust of stars.
Dimnesses drowse. Trust freights pheromonal swarms,
but this night country you are borders on fear
that two breaths may cease to keep one time. Beauty:
sleep – whose Beast is me prised from you, you from me.

II

From you, I'm discerning how to set my range
with myself – that part we show, that part we hide
a subtle moon swinging tight on its hinging
mass: what those who think they know us know us by…
I see now that all things here might seem estranged,
yet every single one is spun with desire
to coalesce – just as you do, sweeter self,
who, being so yourself, become something else.

III

A beach without its sand. Glove without the hand.
Brick, but no mortar. *Cadabra* – no *Abra*.
A shell without its yolk. Boy without the man.
Nations bereft of folk. Love lacking lover
is moon without sun. I could go on. And on.
Only this: each day, at some point or other,
while you're lost in a book, smothering a chair,
I'll sneak a look at you, just to check I'm here.

IV

Love. That four-lettered feather, the half-winged bird
that must chant, alone, the dawn chorus of all
my Beloved is and does. *Live!* with *Oh!* merged
to fledge a lone dove that either swoops or stalls
but slows each world a lover is to one word.
If only we sang it once: a deathbed trill,
a sparrow-burst on last breath… Till then, I'll claim
the best of terms for Love – and murmur your name.

V

Money is everywhere – all over me as
logos I barely chose. Its tart aroma
taints my clothes, still hanging there when I've undressed.
Each part of me, each thought, tinged green by dollars.
Cold cash: secret lover unloved spouses sense.
How can one be faithful, valued by the hour?
But love, you shrug from the shower debt-free, dawn
-minted, your disinterested wet skin-warmed.

VI

I'll steal to you, asleep – will save you till last,
as though I were child to the meal our day is.
Our bed's a cell to the world's body, sweet-dark –
the world, a dark cell to your body. You'll seize
me to you, still in dream, my stiff tremors fast
through you, until you thaw me and, both, we rise
as flesh dough. Yet I hold back, sleep-spurned, cold-baked…
What chill hunger in me tries so not to burn?

VII

There is to some weathers, too rare, that quiet
in paper – as if all this walking world were
watermark to an unseen ream. Can I let
that enter between us, in me, when I dare
what seems change but rages as another *stet*
that turns my drizzling words surreptitious storm?
I've dreamed behind glass: panes childhood puttied in.
These, love, ease free – till home's weather, weather skin.

VIII

I'm beginning to see – to hear, touch, taste, smell –
that to query Love through words gives half-answers.
Nor is louder Love its act: that can be well
and water – or another thirst for clamour.
The self is resonator, all flesh a bell
struck and struck again to wake each mind to prayer.
By all means, then, I'll speak. And kneel before you
till cells – vocal, voiceless – tell me what to do.

IX

Everything in me is on its way to you.
Bus, train, car, plane account for just this: body:
vehicle for a cosmic wanderlust that grew
our bounty – dust. There is something near-godly
in that powerlessness of space, whose each cube
must yield to make dear absence presence. Coldly,
train, bus, plane shoal these cells away – but salmon
soul leaps those currents, returns to you, upstream.

X

What if you should find yourself bereft, death in
cleft mood hearsing me, not you, leaving intact
my better part – you – my mirror's silvering?
Will I have left you a form of verse lacking
nothing of us, clearer than water brimming
air, that shapes me to you, all but breathes me, back –
words as tactile as a palm on the shoulder
or, on your nape, through stillest black, this whisper?

XI

I have made a dreadful mistake. I thought you
you. But you're this head of cloud I wake to, wrung
hair stranded grey, combed down to rain. And its blue
bed too. Sunlight makes everything itself, slung
long and low with shadow, or plainly through noon.
Shall I call you Sun, then? Moon? Things can be one
without resemblance. Thus are you everywhere,
nowhere, at once – whenever absent, most there?

Love-dust

I

See how nature aspires to air. Larva
to butterfly. Or larva to spider,
spider to thrush. Even that hush, vital
within each far ridge of trees, is air's dough
rising with, then to, its weather. We leave
earth because we must – these bodies undone,
for all their seizing – become that striving,
outward, upward thrust. So we rise, though dust.
Flightlessness is that first wise urge for air
held back by fear. Of what? Falling? I fell:
fledglings have no choice – they can only stall
that moment the flightless ignore, or bear.
My heart stirs, egg-heavy. On our nest – hail.
All this downwardness cannot keep us here.

II

See how lavas tend to bedrock. These seas
our motes first met in, now stand at, hands fused,
aren't just our planet's watery stock but
sorrow's vapours, beyond tears, manifest.
Earth is flux fixed. Rock is what our sand mused
upon, refused to shift, brought down on us
till we run for flight. For now, we walk it.
Our love is contained, strained, tectonic with
edges – or parts beds of invisibles
to rifts that swallow, one gulp, an ocean.
Earth is matterlessness brimming extinction,
shy for a reason with love's oil, gas, coal.
I can't yet flow; but offer a heart burned
in its seam, black and rich and potential.

how I wake

or woke once
sensing myself strange
beside you

before brain
could wink I turned
to face you

saw that look
of your own making
hung there in darkness

eyes unblinking
burnt black with love

how many mortals awaking
find themselves so
or fail to sleep

as I do now in dimmest light
your eyes unopened
here beside me

with another's love
aglow in your face – how
on all this whitewashed earth

my love
to keep you
to reap that look?

as if I were out
walking fast
through midnight snow

the only one
stopped suddenly
looking up to find that

full round face prising me
to break me with its gaze
to see me at last

as you did
so fierce in its eyes
electric and awake

& the scales

fell up to my eyes
grey
flurry of ice arising

from dust
glinting heat : a swirl
of wasp

corpses
narrowing through air
growing

thick &
dark to resolve there to
fuse lids

over vision
for tongue was afire with
hurts I had

to say &
all at once that bile-sap in
me had risen

from seeming
death – though there came
to me no sense

no God nor
Saviour no kindly inner
hand – only

the virile sun against
my neck
&

at a gallop that
hot beast
I

was riding

I and You

as we
size ourselves up
as two

-faced :
that man rising in your
woman

the woman
shook to my manly base
though no

dishonesty
here since truth is mostly
glare each

in love must
mirror to another : that
hurt boy

staring through your
look bruised to
its soul

by coldly toying
words or my
girl long

-used in
me I melt to
believing self lone

in my curt
room – these stuck siblings
love carries

as fra-
-gmentary sum
to which all love is wisely yet

only part-
answer : thence
mind undone or unbuckled

swooned to
reflection & this
one heart ever seeking

itself
behind wrecked &
wrecking

eyes

when you

press in
heavy with duvet
close & closer till bodies

sigh one figure
with nothing to say but
a kiss in intensity that comes from

some lingering else
& I know something passed
through you : a memory that tears inside

as a fox frighted or that
story you wear ragged through
night unknown even to yourself – though

all I have of it is this
made so differently in dawn's
wet light : a kiss unearthed dreadless

from our subsoiled
bed presented as if its one
coin untarnished undated were all

that remained
of your great abandoned
civilisation

Backward

you turn it to me
that flecked back with nightfulness in me
starting towards you
lying together but apart

this body slides up to you
blackly tectonic so
softened by love
only to find you no longer temperate

time and again I
reach for you – spine rocky with vertebrae
your *Cape of No Hope* lean and long
hip a stolid island
to beach the small ship of my palm

turn back my love
please face costive fingers these
soundless hands now lost in your hinterlands
more bound and lost than birds grounded in backwaters
they nightly glean to the inch where
life is hard

now my only future
turns its back as though it were yours
never quite here yet heavy with flinching dark beside me

or glimpsed one last time fast receding
lithe and suddenly unfamiliar weaving the crowd
with another's hand at rest
loud on its waist

Same

Did you sleep well? you ask
but it isn't quite the same
With a single *No* all sleep
ungelled in me

Our eyes scan the question
but don't quite rhyme

You move through the house
getting ready – your body
fresh with the world your
body a word spoken for the first time

To your hip to those
slender hips where all my journeys came
it isn't my hand reaching

The smile you just gave our daughter
is only the two of you

That calm in your eyes is water
a shocking drench of water
locking me under

There's balm in you
strong enough to buoy winter light
You're stretching in the hall for days
buoyant with rightness

My night blood stalls in me

The press of your lips is slant
a ballast not quite set

You pull the front door behind you
tight to its frame to
a crack to
a dagger of dark honed to nothing   say
Bye Love
I say it back
but it doesn't sound the same

Invisible Man

Everyone else sees me. You keep
your cat-woman looking laptopped,
caught up in little jerks of mouse. You

spot the black raisin on murky carpet.
I'm disappearing. My sleepless hair is
a lone hat adrift in our house. I'm a tie

disembodied, a flicking wasp of cigarette.
My gel of see-throughness fazes you,
ripples down the hall, disturbing contours.

You hear but can't quite locate me.
Guess where I am. Never ask. Those
far-off eyes now dwell on him, opaque.

Your glance, always a near-miss. It once
was Robin Hood's surest shot, splitting
the bull's-eyed arrow of my gaze.

I should paint myself bright red. Instead
I ghost night rooms – a humming wound.
Unknown by you, my left hand shakes.

I make of myself full transparency. Slowly,
unwind this bandage I've become
until you won't see me at all.

Saint Helena

I'm no sly Napoleon but I
was an emperor once
in her eyes

That kind of emperor
history doesn't deliver –
no hell-bent conqueror

but a visitor her cells
swarmed towards in allegiance
mutually disarmed

Both subject (each supreme)
we marched in calm formation
our daughter at the head

to win that nation of a family
until the slaughters: one by one
our battles crudely came to find us

too defended – some I won
but now in every confrontation
I see our dead accrued

So on this distant island I
watch breath in its air imitate
sweeps of Atlantic cloud

while my retinue of regrets
cannot keep me warm in this
silent house loud with grief

and my physician arriving late
marks death in my deepening
masks of face then asks after

my health – so I query cold seas
so bold on my shore whether
I should dictate a book

whose one subject would be
how with her by my side I might
at last have conquered myself

though she was vaster to me than
any singing burning Russia and now
shook to my blood I must conquer

alone and surrender where no wise
servants come to dry night-rimmed eyes
nor mirror return anything but her look

Tomb

The boulder – old with grief
wide as a moon brought to earth.
One side warm. The other cold.

Outside: breaths of farmhands hang
as they stride through looms of shadow.
For them it is daybreak. Here in this

stone room yellow light never slakes
it has been three years. She ascended
into night. Took brightness with her.

I thought her a saviour. Now I desire
that wound in her perfect body. I'd try
a finger. A thumb. Deep inside her.

Was that healing blood Eve's or Adam's?
I'd have risen with her but she found me
heavy. Or did she sink under her own

slim weight? Resurrection is such a lone
affair. I stink of bone. Our pristine sheet
lies folded and hateful. I hold myself

here blinking the thought of bare feet.
Her betraying kiss. All that smileless talk
of fathers and lovers. All this lame spirit.

I want to see again her fluid walk. Hear
my name borne up on her flesh gasp. Where
is the body? I want the prayer of her body.

Lazarus

There are things perhaps
a father should not write –
how his five-year-old clings
through night in fits of sleep

almost as a woman might
to the man lost in grief
stroking his face his feet
caressing him back to life.

And what if that Lazarus
whose absent wife brought
no tenderness to his tomb
who died alive awaiting

the lover's Pentecost
felt his doomed body visited
in stupor of emergent death
not by the man of the Cross

but by innocent son
by spotless daughter
who melt a stiffened heart
and stir the stifled breath?

Prometheus

you were a woman once
lofty with mildness
such softness in your belly

your avian eyes wild with ocean
locked mine as we
shook with love

I took fire –
a stained dove flown
into that flame of myself

I desired your goddess heat too
completely – showed myself
too human

taut with water I
became a white wave unheard
far out – splashing salt across your
suppleness for your night heart
for that one bird cry

now you have become feather
and talon
your lips stiffen to keratin
those long bones lighter than air

through losing sleep I toss – liver
untouched
bright-yellowed to fennel-bloom

when your eyes refuse to meet
you dive beak-first – gore into me

unrested I nest your head jerking
brow-deep in my chest while
still in this bed
you who bore our child
have left for another man

that other man

again you finish with me to
soar unsated to him your
fluttering speck tan against gloom
disappearing

you will never finish
with him

in slack defeat
I splay on my rock

but fibre by fibre
my devoured heart
however black
grows back –
it beats

it beats

over

I'm a man
giving birth
or stillbirth

of myself
weeping blood
bleeding tears

I blame
that woman
out in the hall

puffing cigars
whose pungent seed
whose buckled dream

planted this
I can't go on
have no shame

any stranger
can stroll into this
scrubbed-down

room of my heart
and see everything
can point casually

to my spread-
apart most intimate
struck-within-me

pain
and murmur
their mild suggestion

but I don't
care anymore
for answers or

questions for
lover or life or
father earth I

just want her
stuck-in thing
that

self-harmed
moonchild
out   I

want this
funeral
birth

over

Grass

I have a solemn wish to be grass

Green
forever vowed to itself irresistible yet
barely seen

except when valued as mild squares –
tended then with blades each Sunday spent
laid out dreaming affairs half-alive half
-married even

How I'd thrive when dead
my wealth shallowly wild in sun's high torpor
sending up green to unburn the planet to countermand
yellow only to turn yellow myself

Watch how a home will pack its trunk
with daughters and sons driven the joyless miles to
grass to sit to shed crumbs and forget what they came for
as even the wise child among them slack on her
vegetable bed absent-mindedly destroys
the sweetly secret seedheads

See if you are able
how it can never hide how
slowly it glides upwards by tiny degree
achieving no great height so towering
legs may stride and lofty eyes read
or unfurrowed brow meditate

Watch the man wheeling and
drunk on dregs relieve himself
into the gratitude he stands upon

or the lone woman who as a teen
unbearably held hands in it now
scuff at it cursing the heel
the tear in the stocking

Yet who on this sacred rock
would don fresh clothes to walk
alone in pairs or with dogs a mound
of gentle shifting earth
ungrassed?

So let me be that sap
they found or put underfoot –
any who loved me and any who don't

my best soon forgotten if beheld at all
so I may grow knitting self to self welding myself
in soft green welts knowing that even those who
sit on me who nestle in me close enough to
smell the noon and swill and shit in me
who then get up and walk on me

wouldn't have walked anywhere else

The loveless lover

based on Lorca's 'The Faithless Wife'

She led me to my river as though
I were a virgin yet already her lover.
It was the one night of the year – that

only night the stars shone. No: not stars
but two lone planets. Venus. Jupiter. Sharp
and unwinking. Edging together in wedded gloom.

Drifting in and out of earshot: tinkling water.
It was my truer self she led me to. Through rippling
clarity I saw what no one sees in darkness: my riverbed's

brazen stones. Far off the yellow lights
of town went out. All around us the crickets lit their
tiny candles of sound. At last I found her slumbering breasts

and they swelled at my fumbling
as hyacinths to spring's first touch. Unseeing
the other we each looked with darkness. Yes she took me as if she

were virgin. These fingers now idle in
love grew fresh with her flaring perfume. The starch
in her flesh drained out – her breath suddenly a petticoat rent by

a dozen shears. Without the moon on her
her canopy of hair was night larch I lost myself in.
We seemed never to end. Again she and I became bright

with undressing – undressing to Us
beside blackberries among the wide and
supple grasses. Beneath her billowing hair I scraped

a pillow of sand: little mound
in which I hid my reddened turtle egg
this buried lobster clicking claws so she'd hear

my slow-ticking heart. I removed
my tie. She took off her skin. We dropped
all weapons. All protection. She took my knife to knotted

ties of corset. My palms had never seen
such skin. My tongue slipped within to her unbearable
sheen of a shell's insides – thighs startling from my lips like fish

at a bell. She was all fire all snow. I could
not but ride as a caveman rode primal mare without bridle
or stirrup. But I am a gentleman and dare not tell those things she

gasped in bright distress. We came away
dress stiff with sand her face worn flush by misfired
kisses. I clasped both hands. I led her from clear trickling water.

Purple blades of iris hacked at space
swaying illusion. I am what I am: that fearless
bounder who lacks and loves with every atom. For her I made

of myself a faded basket she could take with her a massive
straw-made basket she might roundly
give to a husband: that jaded

luster who never noticed. Oh how I fell for her
heart and liver. I did not fall. She
was her own husband

and I just a virgin she called to her river.

& if this snow

could fall so mute
within or clouds muster
columns as lungs

pinked in sunset
or flusters of rain quick with
Ligurian heat could

flurry through veins
just as eyes unseen might rink
with freezing blame

or one could reify
Saharan sand that flights half
-way to conscious sky

broils of worry
insanely reddened – if all
weathers could

truly arise inside
so too must palest blue
or as now

your kiss
imagined in tenderly
insistent snow

quiet
just beyond
my midnight pane